Forty Days

Jenni DeWitt

ALSO BY JENNI DEWITT

Why Won't God Talk to Me?
Surprising Ways He Already Is

Forty Days

A MEMOIR OF OUR TIME IN THE DESERT OF CHILDHOOD CANCER

JENNI DEWITT

Dewitt, Jenni.

Forty Days: A Memoir of Our Time in the Desert of Childhood Cancer. -- 1st edition.

ISBN-13: 978-1501082702

ISBN-10: 1501082701

To all families who are affected
by childhood cancer.

ACKNOWLEDGEMENTS

Thank you, Justin, for living this story by my side and for loving me even on my crazy days.

Thank you, Anthony and Cooper, for being the best kids I could ever imagine.

Thank you, Mom and Dad, for always being my biggest advocates.

Thank you, Mary Thieman, for watching our little darlings while I wrote.

Thank you, Alison Kern, Dawna Nelson, and Tami Heitland, for your gentle nudges and expert advice while editing.

Thank you, Kimberly Mueller-Malone, for your legal advice.

And thank you to each and every one of you who encouraged me to write our story, especially my Grandpa Rollie who kept asking me if the book was done yet.

Contents

Chapter One

Basketball Fever

"Come on boys, hurry up, we are going to be late!" We are always late, but I still wasn't going to give up the dream. The smell of French fries missing in action drifted up from the crevices of our minivan as I watched Tony pull the seatbelt across his little body.

It was winter, 2012, and the cold February air was biting at my bare hands. Hurrying to get Cooper strapped into his 5-point harness, I thought to myself, "Maybe someday I'll be the sort of person who remembers to wear gloves."

Then I lunged for the driver's seat and shut the door quickly against the cold.

Tony and Cooper are 4 days short of 3 years apart and the spitting image of each other, with the exception of the eyes. They were both blessed with my husband Justin's big, beautiful eyes and long lashes, but where Tony's eyes are brown like his daddy's, Cooper's are crystal blue like mine.

Kneeling on the seat, I turned around to give their seat belts one last tug as I said in an overly perky voice, "Safety check!" My friends laugh at what an overprotective mother I am, but I don't let that stop me.

I crossed myself as I started to say my usual prayer for safe travels. All day long I had been fighting a feeling of dread. When I let my guard down, it would start pulling at my arm. Now that I was in the car it was settling more into my thoughts: "Death is lurking." It made my skin crawl.

What if we were going to get in a car crash and die or something? Is this the sort of feeling people have before they set out for the last time? But surely I was being ridiculous. It was just a bad combination of hormones and anxiety, and there was no sense letting a bad feeling ruin our fun.

Glancing at the boys, who were peacefully watching their DVD player, I decided to make good use of the rare quiet to call a few friends. After several messages and hours of great girl talk, I said a thank-you prayer as we pulled into the McDonald's parking lot. Despite my feelings of dread, we had arrived safely at our destination – Wayne, Nebraska – where we planned to watch my husband coach in the girls' basketball district championship.

"See," I told myself, "more proof you were just being silly and worried for no reason. We made it here just fine!"

The snow crunched under my tires as I pulled up next to my parents' old Jeep in the parking lot. We had intended to sit inside and eat, but of course I was running late so there would be no time for that. Mom climbed in the passenger seat as Dad opened the sliding door and made his way to the back seat through a minefield of blankets and discarded sippies.

Their arrival was enough to break the TV trance, and the boys' faces lit up with joy. Both of them started talking at once in their typical efforts to get Grandpa's undivided attention.

Putting the van in reverse, we began making our way the short distance to the McDonald's drive-through. As I handed over my credit card, my mind was on the clock. We should still be able to make it before the game started.

Luckily, that night, I had my parents there to help me keep an eye on the boys. Maybe I would actually get to see a little bit of the game for once.

There is no good place to change a diaper at a basketball game, so as we pulled up to the stadium I decided it might be best to just take care of it in the cramped space of the van.

As I was changing Cooper's diaper I said, "Mom, look at these weird red spots. They are right where the elastic of his diaper rubs."

The rash had been going on for several days, and it seemed to be spreading. It was little red spots that looked like they should be raised bumps, but when I rubbed my finger over them they felt smooth.

Earlier that day I had called the doctor's office to ask if Cooper needed to be seen for the rash. They said it would be a good idea, so we set up an appointment to have it looked at the next day. At least the bumps didn't seem to be bothering Cooper at the moment.

With quick efficiency, I finished changing Cooper's diaper and grabbed some sanitizer before crawling out the sliding door. The smell of the popcorn was inviting as we stepped inside the stadium, and the bright lights got my blood pumping.

I flashed my pass that said I was a coach's wife, and then moved beyond the table to search for a seat. We settled on a spot close to the entrance of the gym. Cooper charmed people with his big blue eyes as they walked in the gym, giving them a high five as they passed.

Warm-ups were in full swing, and the girls were making baskets left and right. Whipping out my mini hand sanitizer, the boys and my parents dutifully held out their hands so I could douse them appropriately with sanitizer before they ate.

I settled the boys at our feet, using the bleacher in front of them as a table. Shortly after the National Anthem, Mom commented, "Cooper sure didn't eat much." Oh well, I thought, he's probably just distracted with such a fun atmosphere.

I had given Tony my old camera to use to take pictures. In addition to the million pictures of his Happy Meal toy, Tony snapped a few pictures of Cooper on my dad's shoulders with my mom in front of them.

That picture would be one of the last "normal" family photos we would take for quite a while.

Chapter Two

Doctor Mom

When it was time to leave, we headed to my parents' house just 10 miles away. I planned to spend the night and drive home in the morning. It was better than making the long drive home alone in the dark.

The boys were wound up with that last burst of energy that screams, *"I'm exhausted, and I have to run around like a maniac or I might accidentally fall asleep!"*

I tried to grab Cooper as he ran by me with all the evasive skills of a 2-year-old. With a concerned look on her face, Mom said, "Look, he's limping a little bit again."

"Cooper, come here a minute. I want to look at your foot." I said.

Mom and I took turns moving his foot around and pushing on different places asking, "Cooper, does that hurt? Does anything hurt?"

"No!" he exclaimed, wiggling in an attempt to get out of my arms and run free. Shrugging my shoulders, I took advantage of his moment of captivity to get him dressed for bed.

Meanwhile, Mom pulled out a gigantic book I hadn't seen since childhood – *The Medical Advisor: The Complete Guide to Alternative & Conventional Treatments* by Time-Life Books. Long ago, in a land far, far away, before the invention of the Internet, this book was Mom's standard reference.

Whenever my sister or I had something physically weird going on, Mom would pull out this huge book and thumb through the pages, playing Dr. Mom while she decided whether or not to take us to the actual doctor.

A few minutes later, Mom had a couple of diagnoses waiting for me regarding Cooper's weird rash. Corralling him for a moment so we could compare and contrast, we agreed that none of the pictures were quite right.

While she continued her search for a diagnosis, I finished getting the boys ready for bed. Then I flipped off the overhead light and turned on a lamp, hoping the dim light would help the boys get the message that it was almost bedtime.

Mom was sitting in the corner with her laptop propped precariously on her knees. "OK, Jen, what about this?" I leaned over her shoulder and squinted trying to read the screen. "Here," she said as she stood up and handed me the laptop. "I'm going to try to get these maniacs to sleep."

I settled in to read, as I became the second generation of Dr. Mom. On the first tab Mom had pulled up, the information was about petechiae. The rash in the picture looked exactly like Cooper's, and the description sounded about right.

Apparently petechiae occur when capillaries, the smallest part of a blood vessel, burst. So my eyes moved to possible causes. I felt a little relief as I saw that non-steroidal medications (aka that boatload of ibuprofen I had given him the week before when we couldn't get his fever to go away) could sometimes cause petechiae. That was probably it.

As I read down the list of possible causes, I saw the word *cancer*. Don't Internet health sites always say cancer? The website advised, "If you have petechiae you should go to the emergency room right away." But didn't the Internet always say that, too?

For once I was going to be a reasonable mom. No sense getting scared by the Internet. After all, Cooper had an appointment the very next day with our own doctor, whom we knew and trusted.

Mom was making progress getting the boys calmed down. Tony's eyes were finally looking a little droopy, so I left him with Mom and headed upstairs with Cooper. Mom had the Pack-n-Play all set up in the spare bedroom.

I hugged Cooper close while I sang him the silly bedtime song he loves so much: *"Lullaby, kiss goodnight, in the glow of the nightlight. Lay down sleepy head, in Cooper's soft bed."*

With his precious green blanket, aptly named Greenie, snuggled in his arms, I laid him down on the fresh sheets. No self-respecting 2-

year-old would go down without a fight, so he fussed for a little bit but soon gave in and dozed off.

The next morning I woke up hearing Cooper's voice calling for Mommy from his Pack-n-Play at the foot of my bed. It wasn't quite time to get up yet, so I brought him to bed with me, and we snuggled close under the warm blankets.

My parent's turn-of-the-century house was solidly built, but the heater didn't quite have enough gumption to compete with the cold Nebraska winters. There was a chill in the air, making our warm bed hard to abandon.

Finally finding the ambition, although maybe not the desire, I decided it was time to get up. I pulled the blankets back and scooped Cooper's little body into my arms.

Heading downstairs we embarked on our morning ritual of chaos as we attempted to get ready for the day. In their frenzy the night before, the boys had sprinkled toys throughout the living room and dining room.

I insisted we needed to pick them up before we left, and Cooper was graciously pretending to help, although nothing seemed to actually be making its way back into the toy bin.

Giggling, he took off running, but was stopped short when he tripped on a toy and fell to the floor on top of another toy. Crying, he ran to me for comfort. I hugged him while I arched my neck to look at the back of his thigh where he had fallen.

My stomach knotted as I saw an unusual, deep-purple bruise forming. There was no way that tiny fall should have left such a mark on my baby. No, that definitely wasn't normal.

As his screams of pain quickly subsided, I carried him in to show my mom. "Mom, look at this bruise. Isn't that weird? He just slipped and fell on a toy."

"Hmm, that is weird." she replied, "Well, take him to the doctor and see what they say."

A half hour later we headed out, behind schedule of course. I had promised my friend that I would pick up her little boy at daycare and drop him off at school. I was going to have to make good time if I didn't want to be late.

Chapter Three

Heading Home

About an hour into my trip, I was annoyed as it started to snow lightly. I hated driving in bad weather. The family joke is, "If there's a flake in the air, Jenni's not going." I gripped the steering wheel a little tighter and let up on the gas.

Gloomily, I thought, "Maybe we are going to get in that car crash after all." But I said another prayer for safe travels, and pushed the negative thoughts out of my mind.

A few hours later we pulled into our

hometown of Albion without a moment to spare. I ran to the door of the daycare to grab my friend's little boy. He chatted happily in the back seat with my boys while I drove the few blocks to preschool.

After dropping off the older boys, Cooper and I headed home. It was naptime, and I had a little work to do before we headed for Cooper's doctor appointment. I had just started working from home transcribing medical records for the local hospital, and I was still learning the ropes.

I tried to ignore the new red spots on Cooper's chubby thighs as I changed his diaper and laid him in his crib. Then I sprinted downstairs to finish my work before we had to leave.

I could hear Cooper crying, and my head was saying, "Leave him. He is old enough to go to sleep without being rocked or cuddled. They do it all the time at daycare, and you have work to do."

But my heart was telling me, "Your baby is crying, go pick him up!" Not surprisingly, after a few moments, my heart won that battle and I shot upstairs. Walking into his room, I was greeted by the familiar smell of baby lotion and well-loved stuffed animals.

We had recently moved Cooper in to share a bedroom with his 5-year-old brother, Tony. It wasn't necessary. We had enough bedrooms for both of them, but I wanted them to have the experience of sharing a room.

I wanted the sound of giggles and goofiness to drift down the stairs at night as they lay awake talking when they were supposed to be sleeping. I dreamed of them being lifelong best friends, and I wanted to do everything possible to foster that relationship.

As I walked in the room, Cooper was standing in his crib, red-faced and irritated. Reaching down I grabbed him and pulled him in close. Relaxing into the old tan rocking chair next to his crib, we both enjoyed the comfort of the cuddles.

He had just turned two, and I knew that the crib and my years of having a baby would soon be on their way out. Rocking back and forth and breathing in the smell of his hair, I was glad I had ignored my work for a moment. It didn't take long before he was drifting off to sleep, and I gingerly laid him down in his crib before bolting back downstairs to finish my work.

Thirty minutes later, it was time to wake him up from his nap so we could leave. For a moment I considered cancelling the appointment. I thought to myself, "Wouldn't it be better if he just got some rest? His body could probably fight off whatever it was."

Besides, I had let him stay up way too late the night before. He needed his sleep now. Plus, Justin told me I was crazy for taking him to the doctor just for a little rash and a limp. After all, the spots weren't even bothering Cooper. He probably just hurt his foot messing around in his crib before he fell asleep a few nights ago. That's why he was limping.

As my hand reached for the phone to cancel our appointment, my feet took over and carried me upstairs to go wake up Cooper.

Nothing runs quickly at a doctor's office, and after a long wait, the doctor finally walked into the room. Nervously I told him, "You're probably going to tell me I'm crazy. I can't put my finger on it; I just think something might be wrong."

Dr. Hupp was in his late 30s with a boatload of his own kids at home, and shaggy hair combed over to the side. Although he exhibited the typical cool-under-pressure doctor persona, I always got a sense that there was a wild rocker dude just under the surface.

With textbook compassion he said, "Well, Jenni, I'm certainly not going to tell you you're crazy. Why don't you tell me a little bit about what's been going on."

More quickly than I intended, words erupted out of me, "He just has this weird rash, I think it might be petechiae. And he's limping, but he didn't hurt himself as far as I know. But he messes around at bedtime in his crib so maybe he hurt it then. He doesn't seem bothered by it though. It's just weird. You know, he just got over that fever last week that lasted for seven days. Sometimes he gets a rash when his fever finally breaks."

"Ok, well let's have a look here," he replied in his calm, even tone. I set Cooper on the exam table and stood close so I could offer him comfort. I pointed out the red spots on Cooper's neck where the seat belt rubbed and then showed the doctor the spots in Cooper's diaper area. Remembering the weird purple bruise from that morning, I told him the story of Cooper's fall.

"OK, mm...hmm," Dr. Hupp nodded, listening. "Cooper, can you get down and show me how you walk?" With a little coaxing we got Cooper to walk across the room.

Setting Cooper back on the exam table, Dr. Hupp said, "Well, he definitely has a limp."

Then the doctor manipulated Cooper's foot and felt his tummy. "Jenni, you are absolutely right, I do think that the spots are petechiae. I am guessing we are seeing a delayed reaction to the ibuprofen that you were giving him. His body is likely still just recuperating from whatever virus he was up against. And as you had mentioned, he could have hurt his foot while messing around at bedtime. As I examine him, I certainly am not noticing anything that I would be concerned about in terms of needing an x-ray. I am going to ask that we get a CBC, just a routine blood test, to cover all our bases."

That all made sense to me, and so we headed over to the lab to get Cooper's blood drawn. I used to work onsite at the hospital, and every day I walked by the lab to get my coffee. It felt odd to be there now as the mother of a patient.

It was getting to be late afternoon, and the flow of patients was slowing down, so we were the only ones in the waiting room. The lady at the desk (I always forgot her name) came out and talked to us. She touched Cooper's hands and face, and all I could think of was how many sick people she came in contact with that day. Now she was touching my *baby*.

Why did she have to be all up in our face? Step back, woman! But I didn't want to be rude so I smiled and made small talk. There was a TV on, and I tried to use it to distract Cooper while I swayed and he wiggled in my arms, antsy to be set free.

Finally, they called us back for the blood draw. I wasn't sure what we had been waiting for since we were the only patients in sight, but at least it was finally our turn. I sat down in the chair with the table attached to it.

I tried to hold Cooper still while they poked his finger and then milked the blood into the tiny vial. I was grateful it filled so quickly. When she was done, I cuddled Cooper and soothed away his pain.

The lab lady gave me a cotton ball to hold on the spot where she had poked Cooper's finger. By the time she was done filling out the information on the vial of blood, the cotton ball was completely soaked. Giving me more cotton balls and gauze she said, "Make sure you are holding it tight and higher than his heart if you can."

Awkwardly holding Cooper, his finger, and my purse, we headed back to our room at the clinic to wait for the results. I paced and bounced as I squeezed Cooper's finger, singing and talking in an effort to distract him.

Chapter Four

The C-word

What was taking so long? I was getting frustrated. It had been over an hour since they drew the labs. Justin was watching Tony for me, but he had a basketball game to coach that night. I needed to be getting Tony so Justin could focus on the game.

That morning, at my parent's house, I had chosen to wear a red shirt, Boone Central's colors, so I would be ready for the game that afternoon. Now I was glad I did, because the color camouflaged all the blood that was getting on me from where they poked Cooper's finger.

Fifteen minutes later, when I still couldn't get Cooper's finger to stop bleeding, I peeked my head out and told the nurse that I needed help. Three of them were standing around the nurses' station talking, and they all looked at me like maybe I just wasn't trying hard enough.

But our nurse broke free from her conversation and grabbed more gauze from the container in the room. I explained, "I've been squeezing it pretty tight and holding it above his head, but it just won't stop bleeding."

"Let's try some ice, sometimes that helps," she said and left the room to get the ice.

When she got back, the gauze pad had already soaked through, and she said, "Oh wow, he is still really bleeding." With a little more sympathy in her eyes, she helped wipe off the spots where the blood had smudged on Cooper's face.

I thanked her and had the fleeting thought that this would be a familiar scenario soon—the kindness of nurses in our moments of need. The thought left as quickly as it came, and I thought, "That was weird," as I shoved it further out of my mind.

Thirty minutes later, I was still waiting for lab results and still struggling to get Cooper's finger to stop bleeding, but at least it was starting to slow down.

Finally, Dr. Hupp walked in the room carrying a piece of paper. In his forced-calm voice, he said, "Well, Jenni, the lab results came back a little abnormal." My heart sank and my stomach did a flip as I listened to him read me the numbers.

"Can I just look at it?" I asked. I am such a visual person, and I'd seen enough lab results in my work in health information management that I thought I could understand it better if I just looked at it.

"Sure, Jenni," he said, laying it on the desk. With dread, I quickly walked up to the desk and looked at the numbers.

Cooper's white count was 85. Normal is between four and six. "Oh, shit," I said, as all the blood drained from my face.

Dr. Hupp nodded, confessing, "That's exactly what I said when I saw it, Jenni. But this could mean a number of things so I went ahead and called down to Children's in Omaha. They said that it isn't an emergency, but they would like to see you yet tonight."

I looked him right in the eye and said, "OK, so it can mean a number of different things. When you look at a lab result like this, Dr. Hupp, what do you think?"

He bowed his head and said, "Well, Jenni, I think leukemia. It's a cancer of the blood."

Instinctively, I took a step away from him. What? Our family didn't get cancer. We had plenty of other health problems in our family history, but not cancer. I looked at Cooper, still wiggling and pushing off my chest in an attempt to be set free. Hugging him closer I thought, "Cancer?!?" I needed to call Justin.

Dr. Hupp stayed with me in the room while I tried Justin's cell phone, our home phone, and finally the school. Luckily there was a lingering secretary who heard the panic in my voice and offered to go track down Justin.

Seconds stretched into minutes as my eyes stared wide and blank. Then her voice was back on the phone telling me she couldn't find him. I thanked her for trying and hung up.

Just then Justin beeped in on my cell phone, thank God! I hit the button to answer the call and blurted out, "We are at the doctor's office, and they did a blood test. We have to go to

Children's Hospital right away. They think Cooper has cancer."

"Are you kidding?" Of course he knew I wasn't, but what the hell do you say when someone blurts out that kind of news over the phone? His mind had already been on the next basketball game, and now his wife was hysterically telling him his kid had cancer?

Dr. Hupp reached out his hand, and I offered up the phone. Patiently, he answered Justin's questions and then hung up the phone. I looked in horror at Dr. Hupp and said, "His platelets are critically low—what if we get in a car accident along the way? He'll bleed out."

With a chuckle he said, "That's not going to happen." Then he patted my shoulder.

I was terrified.

Chapter Five

The Mad Dash

I clung to Cooper as I speed-walked the two blocks home from the clinic. Going in the back door of our house I shouted, "Justin, where are you?" From upstairs I heard, "We're up here!" I ran up the stairs and into Cooper's old room where Justin was throwing clothes into a suitcase. I was pale and frantic, but the second I saw tears rolling down Justin's face something clicked in my brain. It wasn't my turn to be weak. Not now. Later I could be weak.

I hugged Justin, and he sobbed into my shoulder and then hugged Cooper. The boys were looking at us like we had both lost our minds, but their faces lit up when I told them they could go watch TV.

Tony was big enough to get their favorite show going, and so I left them and went back to help Justin pack. "The doctor said to plan on being there for three days so we need to pack at least enough for three days. I don't know what we are going to do with Tony so let's pack for him too."

We threw random clothes and toiletries into our suitcase and looked at each other with wild-eyed fear.

Running downstairs, we loaded everything up in the van, and buckled in the boys. I put our dog in the back yard and told her to stay. As I whipped open the door to the van, I listened to the cell phone ringing in my ear as I called my mom.

For possibly the first time in her life, Mom did not pick up the phone when I called. I left a message, "Mom, we are headed to Children's Hospital. Call me back when you get this."

She called back seconds later, and I told her, "Remember what we were looking up on the Internet last night? Cooper has the worst thing on the list." Shocked, my mom said, "We'll meet you at the hospital. Drive safe."

"I think I know where the hospital is, but text my sister and ask her to make sure," Justin said. Thank God for him. I had no clue how to get to Omaha, let alone where Children's Hospital was.

Justin wanted to call his parents, but he could hardly talk. He kept getting choked up every time he opened his mouth. So I called. I was the calm one. It was a strange role reversal. Typically I am the one who wears my emotions on my sleeve, and Justin is the down-to-earth person exuding calm control.

We quickly stopped at the school on our way out of town. I called my friend Alison and told her that Cooper wouldn't be at his Kindermusik class that evening. I asked her to pray and told her that we were going to Children's.

As we drove, it began to snow. The roads were getting icy, and we started seeing cars in the ditch. When the sun went down, it only got worse.

It struck me that all my worst fears suddenly seemed to be colliding. Not only were we driving in a winter storm, but also our child with essentially no platelets (the blood component that would stop a wound from bleeding) was strapped in the back seat. How could this be happening?

The kids were hungry. It was suppertime, but I hadn't thought to bring them any food. I scrounged around in my purse and found some fruit snacks for them. They were ecstatic. First extra TV and now fruit snacks for supper—they were having the time of their life.

I looked back at Cooper, happy as a clam in his car seat. It was hard to believe he had cancer. They must have gotten it wrong.

I called my friend at the hospital, an ER nurse, and asked him to look up Cooper's last blood draw. The summer before they had checked counts, because they were worried Cooper's growth curve had dropped off.

I remembered when the results came in the mail; I glanced at them and tossed them into the pile to be filed. But today, I would have given almost anything to see normal numbers on that paper.

As I gripped the phone, I listened to my friend read the results from the previous summer. He told me, "He wouldn't have had the leukemia that long ago. It probably just came on recently. But they've done a lot of research on leukemia, and they have real mild chemo now to treat it."

I clung to those words "mild chemo." It made it almost sound like this was just a cold, and we could treat it and then head back home.

Two hours later, we pulled into the cul-de-sac at the front of Children's Hospital.

We left our car parked in a spot out front, and I held Cooper close as we walked through the rotating doors and into the lobby. To my left I heard water flowing and looked over to see an indoor stream. My jaw dropped. I had dreamt about a stream just like it, but I had not known that it existed. I had seen this stream in my dreams, but I hadn't realized it was a warning of the changes to come.

There was a lady at the desk, so we walked up and said that we were supposed to check into the hospital. With an uninterested glance, she looked at me over her glasses and asked if my son had ever been to Children's Hospital.

"No!" I told her, "We just found out three hours ago that he probably has leukemia."

Expecting sympathy, I got none. She turned to her computer and started clicking keys. I was shocked. She had passed over that information as if I had just said, "It's kind of cold out tonight."

What kind of place was this where kids with cancer seemed to be the norm?

My parents arrived minutes after we did, and they entertained the boys while we filled out the endless stream of paperwork. When we were finished, we hoisted our many bags on our shoulders and our front desk clerk grudgingly showed us to the elevators. She pushed the button for 6th floor, and we were whisked up to our new normal.

She handed us off to the nurses at the front desk, who led us to our room. It was a space full of neutral colors with a big, white metal crib standing like a prison cell in the center of the room. The room had a clean, sterile smell to it.

Beyond the crib was a stiff vinyl couch, pushed up against huge windows that offered a beautiful view of the city. It was dark, and red tail lights streamed down the snowy street below. I didn't know it yet, but I would spend hours gazing out at that view.

The boys swung like monkeys from bars underneath the crib. Tony hung upside down from his knees and his shirt fell down over his face. Cooper held on with his hands and swung back and forth trying to be like his brother.

Our nurse, Lynne, had dark, shoulder-length hair and a kind soul. She sanitized on her way in and out of the room and asked us to do the same. Bustling around the room, she got things situated. My sister arrived and everyone was crying—everyone, that is, except the kids and I.

Our doctor came in. I thought Dr. Jill Beck had the most beautiful amber-colored eyes I had ever seen as I listened to her tell me, "You are in the exact right place to get your baby healthy."

She explained that in the morning they would look at Cooper's blood under a microscope, and then they would know more. At that point, she said they should be able to tell for sure if he had cancer, but she admitted that it was likely he did.

"If it is cancer, will they move us to the cancer floor?" I asked her. I imagined a place like in the movies where a bunch of sad, bald children sat around tables playing puzzles and looking sick.

She replied, "This is the cancer floor."

I clutched Justin's arm, and our heads fell back as if we had been struck.

Intern after intern streamed into our room asking questions and more questions. "What was your pregnancy with Cooper like? Did you have any complications? What is his health history? What is your family's health history?"

As they went on and on, I stood there in my red shirt, wearing my son's blood, and answered them numbly. The sounds of my family crying and my children giggling were playing in the background.

I was in denial. I thought, "Maybe it isn't cancer. Look how healthy he seems. It probably isn't cancer. Dr. Hupp said there were other possibilities."

Dr. Beck told us how lucky we were that our doctor had caught things so early. Later we would find out that some kids, upon diagnosis, arrive by helicopter in critical condition, because their doctors took too long to figure out what was happening.

Chapter Six

The First Night

My mom, dad, and sister Chelsey took Tony and headed to an economy hotel nearby. I listened to the nurses tell me they needed to put a PICC line in Cooper's arm so they could draw blood and give him the medicine he needed.

I nodded my assent and held him down while they poked around in his arm with the needle. He screamed and writhed in pain. I tried talking to him, singing – whatever I could think of to calm him down and distract him – but nothing worked.

As I sat, unsure what to try next, I felt something wet drip on my arm. I looked up and

Justin was standing above me, silently crying at the sight of his son in so much pain.

Finally the nurses found the vein and secured the needle with bandages. Our baby was hooked up to an IV pole getting fluids. It was a leash he would be tied to for the next six weeks.

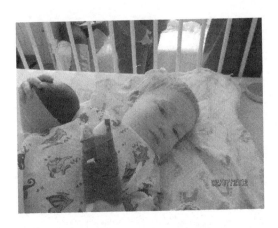

The doctors had told us in the morning they would do a bone marrow biopsy and a spinal tap. Then they would give Cooper his first chemo. But that night it was late, time for bed. I held Cooper and sang his favorite bedtime song to him, trying not to think about how the night before we had been a normal family. Now everything was upside down.

When Cooper drifted off to sleep, Justin and I huddled together on the vinyl couch underneath the big window. The nurse had given us blankets, and I had put them on the couch in a vain attempt to make it feel more like a bed.

There were no words, so we laid in silence. Eventually, I could hear Justin's breathing shift into that slow, rhythmic sound that meant he was asleep. The medical instruments were giving off enough glow that I could see Cooper's tiny shape in the big crib next to us.

Finally, alone in the silence, I let my guard down. Feeling all the terror of the day, I mentally whispered, "God, I'm so scared."

As I gazed down and to my right, I felt God. I didn't hear a thing, but I felt Him tell me, "This is just something you are going through. Everything is going to be OK." Comforted, I settled into that feeling and rested there until I drifted off.

I didn't know it, but that moment would be one that I would cling to for the next nine months as I watched my son endure wave after wave of cancer treatment.

Sometimes – a LOT of the time – I would start to doubt. I would wonder if I could trust that voice I had heard. What if it had just been my own wishful thinking? What if the message had been born of anxiety and exhaustion from the traumatic events I had just endured?

Some days I would be tormented, thinking, "What if I misunderstood? God said it would be OK in the end, but He never told me how bad it would be in the middle. Oh my gosh, what horrible things are going to happen in the middle?"

But that first night, I slept, huddled on the couch with my husband, until Cooper woke up scared a few hours later. Then I crawled into the huge crib with him and held him in my arms. The only way Cooper seemed to be comfortable was when I sat up holding him. Finally, he drifted back to sleep, and I leaned against those cold metal bars and closed my eyes.

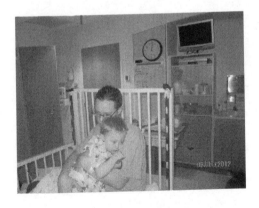

Chapter Seven

CaringBridge

The next morning, February 8, 2012, the doctors confirmed our fears. It was, indeed, leukemia. Treatment would follow a general protocol until we could get the biopsy from the bone marrow back to help us know exactly what kind of leukemia we were dealing with.

While I tried to absorb the information, my phone buzzed with the millionth text of the hour. Our friends were concerned. They wanted to know what was happening and how they could help.

My sister said, "Maybe you should start a CaringBridge site. Then you wouldn't have to be texting the same thing to different people over and over."

I had never heard of CaringBridge, so I asked her what it was. "It's an online journal you can keep updated with what's going on," she explained. "Then people can sign on and read the updates."

Annoyed, I said, "Cooper's not *that* sick; we don't need that." She raised one eyebrow, but then let the subject drop. A few days later, when Justin's sister suggested the same thing, I decided it was time to give in. I was sick of texting.

So I sat on the edge of the giant crib holding Cooper and dictating our story, while Justin's sister, Jesi, set up our CaringBridge site. When we were done, we posted it on Facebook so the world could join us on our journey through hell and back.

Every night, once I got Cooper settled down, I would write about our day. I don't know that I ever gave much thought to it, but early on I instinctively knew that if I wanted people to keep reading (and thus remembering to pray for Cooper), then I needed to write something people would want to read.

Nobody was going to come back day after day to hear, "Well, he puked five times today.

They don't know why his counts aren't coming up. His throat is so raw from the chemo that he can't eat anything." No way!

So I started paying attention to the good things and funny stories that happened throughout the day. Then at night I'd sit on that crappy vinyl couch and write about it. Unwittingly, my CaringBridge essentially became a list of all the things I was grateful for each day. I never could have guessed how therapeutic that would be.

Chapter Eight

The Results

The days dragged on, one blending into the next in a haze of medical procedures and treatments. One day Justin looked at me and said, "Why aren't you crying? You're kind of freaking me out." I didn't know why. I didn't understand why I wasn't crying. There was just a part of me that wouldn't allow it.

Finally, the preliminary results from the bone marrow biopsy came back. Justin held Cooper across the room, and I sat in a cold metal folding chair near the door talking with our doctor and the nurse practitioner.

The doctor explained, "The type of cancer Cooper has is called ALL—acute lymphoblastic leukemia. The treatment plan is mostly outpatient with some inpatient stays." In my head I was trying to remember if ALL was the "good" form of leukemia or the bad one—as if there was such a thing.

They went on to explain that they would give Cooper chemo now to wipe out the cancer, but the medicine couldn't tell the difference between the good cells and the bad ones so it would wipe out both. Once Cooper's daily lab draw showed the cancer was gone and his body started building healthy cells again, then we would be allowed to go home.

Dr. Beck cautioned us that this could take up to four weeks, but she assured us that we would likely be out of the hospital in three weeks.

Linda, the nurse practitioner, was a big woman with thick-rimmed glasses. Her movements were huffy and she seemed to look at you but never really see you. She told me she would teach us how to read the lab results so we could follow Cooper's progress.

I wasn't overjoyed with the prospect of having her as my new teacher, but she seemed like my only choice. And regardless of who was teaching me, I was eager to learn whatever I could about this world we had been thrust into.

They explained that throughout the course of treatment, especially for the first 9 months, Cooper's immune system would be extremely compromised. I asked them question after question about what we needed to do to try to keep Cooper safe.

I remembered hearing that people need exposure to *some* germs to build up the immune system, so I asked them, "Can I keep the room too clean?" I had been compulsively cleaning the room since we arrived, but I didn't want to accidentally slow Cooper's body from building back up healthy cells.

My new teacher, Linda, leaned back and cocked her head to the side with a look that said, "Whew, we got a crazy one here!"

Dr. Beck held her emotions a little better and patiently explained that with Cooper's weakened immune system, exposing him to germs was not going to help him build healthy cells more quickly. However she also assured me that I didn't need to drive myself crazy trying to keep everything sterile.

I didn't know how to explain to her that sitting around doing nothing would make me more crazy than moving around cleaning things. At least the cleaning was *something* I could do to help control a situation where I felt like I had no control.

The doctors gave us a white 3-ring-binder with helpful, overwhelming information, and then they left the room. We weren't sure how much or little to tell the kids, so the social worker came in and tried to help us. Her suggestions were helpful in a general way.

I didn't know if it would help, but I told Cooper that someday he was going to feel better. I assured him that Mommy and Daddy loved him and would be with him. One time I even explained to him that there were other rooms in the hospital with other sick kids. He blinked back up at me, looking intently at my face.

Tony had been bouncing back and forth between my parents' house and Justin's parents. They brought him to the hospital for short visits about once a week, and we talked on the phone as much as a 5-year-old's attention span would allow. We let him spend the night at the hospital when we could. It was comforting to all of us to be together as a family again.

When he came, Tony would give Cooper little presents. Cooper would clutch the presents in his hands for hours after Tony left.

Justin and I were amazed at how well Tony seemed to be handling things. He had never really been away from us for a day, much less weeks on end, but he seemed to be enjoying all the extra time with his grandparents.

We explained to Tony that Cooper had cancer and would have to take a lot of medicine. Then we answered his questions as they came up, trying to keep our answers simple and to the point. Justin was better at that than I was.

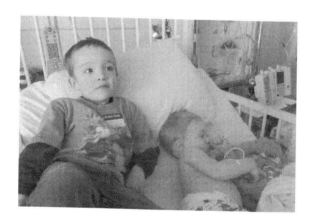

Chapter Nine

Breaking Point

We quickly learned there is no such thing as "mild chemo." The side effects from the medicine caused Cooper to be miserable. At one point, he was so constipated that he was in almost constant pain. In addition, his blood pressure had skyrocketed, and the doctors were having a hard time getting it under control. It was scary, and everyone's feelings were heightened.

Day after day, I sat helplessly in the chair attempting to comfort Cooper while they tried one medicine after another to give him relief. My heart was broken. I longed for the kind of hurts that could be healed with a kiss from Mommy.

One day my mom and dad came for a visit. We sat and talked about things that didn't matter and Mom kept sniffling.

I tried several times to explain how weak Cooper was and that the chemo had completely wiped out his body's ability to fight infection. I hinted that anyone who might be sick should wear a mask just in case, because an infection could be extremely dangerous for Cooper.

To my frustration, Mom wasn't taking my hints. She was convinced that her sniffles were from allergies. While she was probably right, I was already terrified for Cooper's life. Plus, the sleep deprivation and stress of Cooper's constant pain had me on edge.

Finally I blurted out, "Mom, can you please put on a mask just in case? You seem like you have the sniffles."

Standing up quickly, her face flushed with anger, she said, "I knew that's what you were hinting at. Forget it – I'll just leave." And she stormed out of the room.

My mom's family has a history of getting

in fights and then not talking to each other for years, and in my exhaustion I was just sure Mom was done with me.

The thought that my mom would not talk to me through this ordeal sent me over the edge. It was more than I could handle, and my spirit broke. I started weeping in agony, unable to control the sobs as they ripped from my heart and out of my mouth.

Everything that had been heaped on my head finally came crashing down as the dam broke and a flood of tears poured out. Justin came and took Cooper from my arms.

I raced into the bathroom and shut the door in an attempt to muffle the sound of my sobs. After a few minutes, my dad came in and rubbed my back as I knelt on the cold tile floor. My body was racked with anguish as I cried uncontrollably.

It was my weakest moment. I was lost. I literally was at the end of what I could handle. Then I started noticing my hands were tingling and frozen like crab claws. I cried out in fear, "Dad, what's happening to my hands? I can't move my hands!"

"I think you are having an anxiety attack, honey," he said softly.

Appalled that I could be so weak, I started wailing again. Later, in prayer, the Holy Spirit would show me that this moment was when God fled to my aid with such force that I felt it physically in the tingling of my hands. But at that moment, I didn't understand what was happening.

Over the next several minutes, I started to calm down. As I began to relax, a surreal calm spread over me. I felt better than I had in days. And in this peace, I knew that my mom would not quit talking to me; she would always be my biggest advocate. But this was happening to her grandson too, not just my son. It was hard for everyone.

Thirty minutes after my emotional breakdown, our prayers for poop were answered when Cooper finally had his first bowel movement in over ten days. At least for the moment, it seemed to give him some relief.

Chapter Ten

Stepping Away

The days went on. Cooper was still uncomfortable, but his pain wasn't quite as intense. He preferred to have me holding him, but now he would let me set him down without screaming for me the whole time.

It had been almost two weeks since he was diagnosed. Since that day, I had not stepped foot outside of the hospital. People kept trying to convince me that I needed to step away, reminding me this was a marathon – not a race – and I needed to keep my strength up.

At first I was adamant that I would not leave until Cooper did. But Justin kept talking to me, and eventually he convinced me that maybe it would be OK to leave just for a little bit while Cooper was sleeping.

There was nowhere I wanted to go, but I decided maybe church would be an OK choice for my first venture out of the hospital room. Ash Wednesday was fast approaching, and although my friend Lynne wasn't Catholic, she had wanted to go to a Catholic Ash Wednesday service for years. We decided to go together.

Lynne pulled up to the front door of the hospital, and I hesitantly opened the door and climbed into her vehicle. I felt like there was a cord tied on one end to my heart and on the other to Cooper. As she put her foot on the gas pedal gently propelling us forward, the cord tugged uncomfortably at my heart, making me want to shout at her to stop.

I wanted to throw open the door of her car and jump out, flailing my arms like a crazy person as I wildly ran back up to the hospital room, but before I could work up the nerve, we had arrived at the church.

The parking lot was packed, but we finally found a spot at the back and headed to the front door. With a mixture of modern and contemporary decor, the large church looked like it had been built in the 1980s.

We found a seat two-thirds of the way back on the left side and sat down. I clutched my hand sanitizer and prayed no one would give me some illness that I would carry back to Cooper.

As people streamed up to the front of the church first to take Communion and then again to receive ashes on their forehead, I looked at their faces and wondered if they'd had their "worst day." That's how I thought of the day that my baby was diagnosed with cancer. My worst day. A day worse than my wildest imagination.

I looked at their faces, envying the fact that when Mass was over they would go home to their normal lives. They had no idea that it was Armageddon in my world. They were totally unaware of my suffering. And while our circles of reality were overlapping at the moment, they existed in a different world than I did. My world was full of fear and uncertainty, pain and grief. I simultaneously hated them and wanted to be them.

During the church service, Lynne's daughter Evie started crying. Lynne couldn't figure out why, but I was relieved she was crying. Somebody needed to cry; it was all so sad. If she cried, then somehow I didn't have to. Then I could sit there numb, balled up inside myself, nervous and scared.

In the car after the service, Evie told her mom that she had been crying as she thought about Jesus dying on the cross, because she was so sad he had to die for our sins. The faith of a child—it never fails to amaze me.

For a while, after that church service, I started mentally categorizing all people into "Befores" and "Afters" based on whether they'd had their "worst day" or not. In my mind, the Befores had never been through a traumatic event. They were awkward, not knowing what to say to me, and they were overly cheerful in their naiveté. I appreciated their efforts. It meant a lot that they tried, but they just didn't get it.

The Afters, on the other hand, walked around with a shadow on their face. They knew. They'd been there before. They'd had their "worst day," and they had the scars to prove it. Let me tell you, you meet a lot of Afters on the cancer floor at a children's hospital. Those were my people. They were the ones who understood, who hated the words "this is your new normal" as much as I did.

Chapter Eleven

Residents in Training

As our days in the hospital piled up, our understanding grew. We found out that the reason Cooper had been limping when we brought him in was because his bones hurt. How deep must that pain have gone? How tough did God make my baby that when we asked if it hurt he said no?

One day, Cooper went under anesthesia for a spinal tap, but when they tried to do the procedure, there wasn't enough spinal fluid. As the doctors walked across the lobby to give us the bad news, the residents trailed behind with looks of apprehension and horror on their faces.

That's when I learned that if you want to know the truth, you look at the residents. They haven't learned how to smooth the emotion off their faces like the doctors have. They don't know yet how to put the truth in a way that doesn't sound so horrible.

With the calm that comes from experience, the doctors told us that they were not able to get enough spinal fluid and they would try again tomorrow with another spinal tap. They assured us that this was likely just due to some dehydration, so they would give Cooper extra fluids throughout the day to help.

Later, the nursing student who had been observing the spinal tap told us, "That was the most horrible thing I have ever seen. One doctor after another, they just kept poking and poking him, but they couldn't get anything."

I wondered why she would tell us that. Clearly she had forgotten that her patient was our little boy!

Chapter Twelve

The Sanitizer Incident

Unfortunately, since Cooper's repeat spinal tap was being scheduled for the next day, there were no appointments available early in the day. We had to schedule for an appointment at noon, which meant Cooper wouldn't be able to eat from midnight until noon the next day.

His current medication regimen included steroids, which caused the side effect of extreme hunger. In addition, it increased his temper so that his fuse was short and his emotions more extreme than your typical 2-year-old, if you can imagine that.

On the morning of his repeat spinal tap, he woke up saying, "Daddy, donuts?" How do you explain to a 2-year-old that they are fasting for a surgery scheduled later in the day? You don't. So our hungry little Cooper just kept screaming, "Daddy, doooonuuuts!" We tried to distract him the best we could, but nothing worked.

At one point, Justin left to go switch out the laundry down the hall. We didn't know it, but Cooper thought he went to get donuts. When Justin came back into the room empty-handed, Cooper went into a wild fit of steroid rage.

After a few hours, the situation was getting pretty tense. I was shaky with stress and sleep deprivation, not realizing I had forgotten to eat since noon the day before. It was the recipe for a perfect storm.

To add to the stress, the night before, our sanitizer had run out. We used sanitizer practically as often as we drew breath, because Cooper's counts (the part of the blood that helps the body fight infection) were so low and I was so obsessive about trying to keep him safe. I had asked three different nurses to have our sanitizer refilled without any results.

Luckily, we had a small sanitizer of our own to use in the meantime, but to my great annoyance the night nurse had chosen to use that instead of making sure the hospital's dispenser was refilled.

By that morning, the perfect storm came to a head, and I lost it. Our pretty, blonde nurse walked in, and I screamed at her, "Where is our s%&*@+! sanitizer? You all tell me my son has no immune system and that we need to keep things extremely clean, but then you won't bring us any sanitizer! What is going on?!?"

While I spoke, I waved my hands in the air for emphasis, like a crazy person. Somewhere in the back of my brain, Rational Jenni woke up from her nap and told me I was acting like a lunatic, but I simply could not control myself. I stormed out of the room, as our sweet nurse apologized and promised to get us some sanitizer.

Moodily, I trudged down the hall to check the laundry. On my way back, I stopped at the nurses' desk and rudely leaned between the nurse and the nursing student to get sanitizer. As I excessively pumped the nozzle to emphasize my point, the nursing student looked at me with a look that said, "Girl, you are Crazy with a capital 'C'!"

I wanted to rip her a new one and explain that she really had no idea what kind of stress I was under, but by that point I had myself slightly more under control. So instead, I walked into Cooper's room and firmly shut – OK, slammed – the door behind me. Later, I found out that having a nursing student involved with your child's care was optional, so I swiftly opted out.

In our entire stay, that nursing student was the one and only nurse who made me feel judged or looked down upon. I am still in complete awe at the kindness our nurses showed, even in the face of my fits of rage, crying, and overall generalized craziness. I'm praying God heaps rewards on them in Heaven someday.

So we got our sanitizer that morning, Cooper got his spinal at noon, and I ate lunch. Then things seemed a little better.

That afternoon, the janitorial supervisor came and apologized personally to me. She told me, "We checked the phone records. The only time anyone called us to get a refill was this morning when Claire called."

"Great," I thought. "Claire was our pretty, sweet nurse. So I had yelled at the one person who

actually listened to me." Later that day I swallowed my pride and apologized to our precious nurse, Claire. With all the kindness of the Blessed Mother Mary herself, Claire accepted my apology while soothing my bruised ego.

As you can imagine, Cooper got his donuts after surgery.

And the next time he had an inpatient stay, there were signs above the sanitizer dispensers in all the rooms. They gave a phone number you could call if you were having trouble getting your dispenser refilled. Justin laughed and said, "Good job honey, they made a sign for you."

I was a little embarrassed that my temper tantrum had resulted in a sign, but even more than that I was grateful to the hospital. Somehow, they had heard the story of one stressed out mother on sixth floor, and they had addressed the issue. They had done what they could to help alleviate my stress, and I was so very grateful for their kindness.

Chapter Thirteen

Miracles

As time went on, Cooper was in more and more pain. The chemo kept him constipated, and the leukemia made him ache all over.

He spent most of his day cooing and whimpering to himself while I held him, feeling helpless. At one point I wrote in my journal: *"Cooper moans/coos as if to self-comfort. It is the sound I make when I am trying to get him to sleep. Sometimes I make the sound for him hoping he will feel like he can rest. Then I space out and forget to make the sound, and he starts in again."*

I spent most of my time sitting around holding Cooper trying to help him get comfortable. When I set him down so I could go to the bathroom, he would scream for me. I ate all my meals with a teetering plate, trying not to drop food on his head.

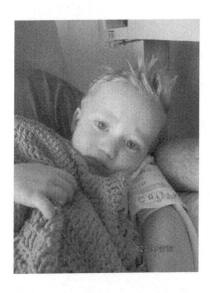

On those long, sedentary days, as I played with Cooper's hair, dreading the day it would fall out, inevitably I would find myself rambling to God. I was trying to pinpoint exactly which sin I had committed that warranted God allowing my baby to get cancer.

I vaguely remembered a part in the Bible that talked about punishing offspring for their parents' mistakes to the third and fourth generation, so I flipped through the Bible looking for clues to where I had gone wrong. But instead of finding the answer to my question, I kept randomly opening my Bible to stories about Jesus healing someone.

After several days of this, I started to wonder what was going on. I never realized how much the Bible talked about healing. I was perplexed. How had I never noticed that before?

Cooper was not getting better, and the doctors were starting to admit that they didn't know why he was still in so much pain. I decided it was time to take a risk and get a second opinion. After all, I had been reading for days about this Guy who could heal Cooper with just words.

So I prayed.

It was the kind of prayer that you scream directly from your heart. I told Jesus that I believed he could heal my son if he wanted to, and I begged him over and over and over to heal Cooper. In the back of my mind, I knew that God was not my magic genie, and He would do whatever He darn well pleased.

But I prayed, because I knew that, if He *wanted* to heal Cooper, He could. There was no flash of lightning or booming voice; we just kept rocking in our crappy vinyl chair.

That afternoon, Cooper seemed to be feeling a little better, so we moved from our chair to the couch by the window. We got all settled in and while Cooper watched Tom and Jerry, I picked up my Bible. Like usual, I opened it to a random page and started reading.

The very first words to meet my eyes were, "Go in peace, your faith has healed you." I thought...could this possibly be God telling me that He had answered my prayer? No way!

I mean, I believed He could do it if he wanted to, but could this really be a sign or was it just a coincidence? That sort of thing only happens in the Bible, right?

Growing up in Nebraska, you get used to the idea that nothing overly important usually takes place in your state. You hear stories about all this stuff that is going on out in the world, but it is somehow separate from you.

I think I kind of view the Bible that way sometimes. There are cool stories, and I believe them, but surely nothing that cool could happen here, right? Wrong.

Cooper seemed to progressively feel better, and I hoped and prayed that maybe the cancer had gone away. We were still waiting to get the results of the bone marrow biopsy taken the week before. It would tell us how well the leukemia was clearing from Cooper's body.

I'll never forget the confused look on the doctor's face when we finally got the results. Her brow furrowed as she told us, "There were some inconsistencies with the results of the previous bone marrow biopsy."

Apparently, when Children's Hospital examined the biopsy sample, it had shown more cancer than it should have for this stage of treatment. However, when they shipped the *same* sample to a hospital on the east coast, around the same time I had prayed so fervently for Cooper's health, it had been found to be essentially cancer-free.

She explained that they would do a third bone marrow biopsy to help get a clearer picture of what was happening, and with that biopsy we would hope to see less than 5% leukemia. According to the doctor, Cooper's prognosis and future treatment would hinge on what we found out with the biopsy.

Later, when the results came back showing 0% leukemia, I smiled. Jesus had healed my baby.

Chapter Fourteen

Bald is Beautiful

You would think I would start to relax. Jesus healed my baby; we were good to go. Not to mention that first night when I felt like God had told me everything would be OK.

But *still* I doubted and worried.

They had warned us that Cooper would be losing his hair soon, and I was dreading the day. I knew it was going to be hard to see him looking like the "cancer child" that he now apparently was.

I'd seen the brochures from St. Jude's Hospital many times, with the bald sick kids smiling on the front. We'd even participated in a fundraiser through the boys' daycare to raise money for the "sick kids," as I called them. But somehow those "sick kids" were always separate from me. It was sad, but it didn't overly affect me.

Now it was my reality. My life. My sick kid. I wrote on CaringBridge:

"Tonight we noticed that Cooper started to lose his hair. Justin actually noticed it first when he looked down and his black BC Lady Cardinals basketball t-shirt had little blonde hairs sticking to it where Cooper's head had been resting."

Part of me wonders if Cooper will actually be relieved to lose his hair since I keep annoying him by

running my fingers through it. They said it could grow back a different texture or color, so I feel the need to try to memorize what it looks like and feels like right now. As a visual aid, I have taken several pictures with a slightly more top-down angle than I normally would!"

Chapter Fifteen

Waiting Game

It was amazing to us that just when Cooper started to lose his hair and really look sick – that's when he started to feel better. Still, we weren't allowed to go home from the hospital. They reminded us that our ticket out was two-fold. The cancer had to be gone AND his body had to start producing new cells. Unfortunately, his body still had not kicked into gear producing healthy cells, and so we waited.

Our hoped-for, three-week discharge date came and went without change. As the fifth week rolled around, we were starting to get really frustrated.

When Cooper's immune system had been wiped out for twice as long as any other kid on the *same* treatment plan, I wondered if I had misunderstood what God was telling me.

During the first few weeks of Cooper's treatment, we had met another family. The mom was so mad at God that her son was sick, and yet things seemed to be progressing ahead of schedule for them.

I had never thought to be mad at God. I was too busy being mad at myself. It was my job to protect my kids, and Cooper had gotten sick. Where had I messed up? What had I done wrong? I'd used the organic products, I'd tried so hard to control everything, and still this had happened.

But here was this mom, so angry at God, and her child was recovering faster than mine. Did I need to consider her tactics? Maybe she was on to something? That week I wrote in my journal:

"I told the doctor, 'Maybe I should just get angry at God. Maybe God would listen to me then?'

She told me, 'You should be angry.' But I tried that hat on and it just didn't seem right. Being mad at God is like being mad at the one person you always go to for help. How can you be mad at them?"

It wasn't until much later in our journey that I became angry at God – furious, actually. And at that point, my priest told me it was important to be honest (respectful, but honest) with God about how I was feeling. He pointed out that God knows everything. He already knew I was mad at Him, and pretending I wasn't was kind of like lying. So I followed his advice. I was honest with God as I prayed, and it was one of the most healing conversations I've ever had.

But I wasn't to that point yet. I was still stuck – stuck in anger at myself and stuck in deep grief. I could hardly bear the devastation at seeing my baby so sick. Linda, the nurse practitioner, admitted to me one day that I didn't seem to be handling things as well as some of the other moms. But I couldn't help it. I didn't know how to separate Cooper's suffering from myself. I felt like I had cancer too. Constantly on CaringBridge I would write things like, "We got chemo today." Then I would backspace and change the "we" to "he."

I continued to have a hard time leaving Cooper. He didn't need me so much for comfort now that he was feeling better, but I couldn't let go of that control and step out. With encouragement from Justin, though, I did force myself to leave sometimes.

I didn't want another "sanitizer incident" as a result of not remembering to take care of myself. So I left, but I stayed close. I usually either went to the Target that I could see from the window of Cooper's hospital room or the church just a few blocks away.

One Sunday, the priest's homily was about another mother he had visited at Children's Hospital. He told of how her baby was dying, and she refused to leave. The priest went on to explain that he tried to get her to leave and just couldn't believe that she would spend days in that hospital room not taking care of herself.

I don't remember what the underlying lesson was supposed to be in his homily. I just remember thinking that he obviously didn't understand the agony a parent feels when their child is suffering. Your needs don't matter; they are a complete non-issue.

In my mind, Mary, Jesus' mother, was the only one who could "get it." After all, she had watched her son suffer though crucifixion. She knew a mother's pain at watching her child suffer. Still, I couldn't help but wonder, if God let

His only son suffer and die, what was He going to let happen to *mine*?

Even though his body didn't seem to want to start making healthy cells, Cooper continued to feel better. At least that was encouraging.

He hadn't been able to walk for several weeks as a result of the illness and days upon days lying around the hospital room. Physical therapy had encouraged us to play "for" him in the hopes that he would feel motivated to start moving again. So Justin and I let the inner child out, building tracks and bouncing balls. He started by holding the ball and driving the train. Then slowly he started to scoot around, and then crawl.

Finally, one sweet day, we were at the toy room playing with Thomas the Train, and Cooper took his FIRST steps...again.

Chapter Sixteen

One More Test

Once he started walking again, Cooper's strength built back up quickly. Soon it was hard to keep him occupied in that tiny little room while he was hooked up to all those tubes. Our hospital stay dragged on as we waited for Cooper's body to start building normal cells.

Every day they would test Cooper's blood to see if the cells had started to build, and every day there was no change. It was getting more and more defeating by the moment. It seemed like we were always waiting to hear back on just one more test. Each time I thought, "If this test is good, maybe I can relax." But I never could.

One day Justin told me, "Jenni, there is always going to be one more test. We are going to spend our life not knowing what the next test will tell us. But we can't get SO worried about the next test that it completely incapacitates us for today."

I stared at him. I knew he was right.

I needed to figure out how to be OK within the day. I couldn't handle the "what ifs" of tomorrow. So instead of wasting time worrying, I tried to spend my energy focusing on today and today only. Whatever was wonderful, whatever was good – that's what I tried to think about.

> *"Finally, brothers and sisters, whatever is true, whatever is noble, whatever is right, whatever is pure, whatever is lovely, whatever is admirable – if anything is excellent or praiseworthy – think about such things." (Philippians 4:8, NIV)*

I felt like the Israelites wandering in the desert. The book of Exodus describes their journey from slavery in Egypt to freedom in the Promised Land of Canaan, a trip that took 40 years. When they complained about being hungry, God made it rain food for them—a type of flaky bread called manna. If they worried about the future and gathered more manna than they needed for that day alone, it rotted in their tents overnight. It was God's way of teaching them to rely on him every day for what they needed.

I imagined what a pain it would have been for the Israelites if God had told them, "OK, here's enough bread for a week." Then they would have had to haul it with them as they walked all week, and it wouldn't have been as fresh as it was the first day.

In the same way, the problems of a week are heavy and awkward to carry. But the problems of a day—they are manageable with God's help. So I tried to trust God to give me the grace and strength I needed for the day at hand. I tried to quit carrying around the worries of the weeks, months, and years to come.

Chapter Seventeen

Walking on Water

Still, I had days where I could feel the anxiety flooding my brain and flipping my stomach. There was a Bible story that would come to mind during those times. It was about Jesus walking on the water. In the story, Jesus' disciples were floating along in their boat when Jesus went out to them, walking on the lake. At first the disciples were terrified. They thought he was a ghost.

> But Jesus immediately said to them: "Take courage! It is I. Don't be afraid."
>
> "Lord, if it's you," Peter replied, "tell me to come to you on the water."

"Come," he said.

Then Peter got down out of the boat, walked on the water and came toward Jesus. But when he saw the wind, he was afraid and, beginning to sink, cried out, "Lord, save me!"

Immediately Jesus reached out His hand and caught him. "You of little faith," He said, "why did you doubt?"

And when they climbed into the boat, the wind died down. Then those who were in the boat worshiped Him, saying, "Truly you are the Son of God."

(Matthew 14:27-33, NIV)

Just like Peter, I felt like I had taken a few steps out in faith. However, it always seemed like my "earth brain" would kick in, and suddenly I would notice the huge waves of life all around me. Then, suddenly, all the reasons I shouldn't trust came flooding back, and I would start sinking down into the waters of fear and anxiety.

In the story, though, when Peter started to sink, he shouted out, "Lord, save me!" Then Jesus reached out his hand and pulled Peter from the waters of doubt and anxiety.

So I borrowed Peter's line. When things got to be too much and I felt myself sinking, I would mentally scream, "Lord, save me!" To my surprise and delight, the Lord came to my rescue again and again.

It was a nice story, but not one that I had shared with anyone. It was strictly between God and me. Then one day I got an email from my cousin. It was a message from her sister-in-law about what her 6-year-old niece had said before bed one night:

I talked to the kids tonight about Cooper and how we needed to keep him and his family in our prayers. I talked briefly about how scared his parents must be when you have a child who is so sick. Madeline said it reminded her of the story of Peter and Jesus when he had Peter walk to him on the water. "He became scared and distracted and took his eyes off Jesus and he started to sink. Cooper's parent's just need to remember to keep their eyes on God and they will be OK.

The email stopped me in my tracks. If I had doubted that God was there with me, if I had wondered if I understood Him correctly, then here, out of the mouths of babes, was my reassurance.

Chapter Eighteen

Just Enjoy the Snow

I started to notice that repeating simple phrases helped me calm down on days when the anxiety was really bad. One day, Justin was planning to go coach district basketball finals in a town a few hours away.

It had been a beautiful day all day. Then, to my horror, an hour before Justin was going to leave for the basketball game it started to snow like crazy. It had been sunny one moment and the next it was practically a blizzard.

With the typical panic that ensues when bad weather and driving collide in my life, I pulled up the weather. On the map, it looked like just a tiny weather system that would pass quickly, but when I looked out the window, it was a blizzard!

I tried to calm myself down, rationalizing that God had taken care of my baby, as sick as he was, and he would take care of my husband. Between deep breaths, I realized that I had never seen the snow fall from 6 stories up. I couldn't believe how magical it was as each flake floated to the ground like a leaf blown in the wind.

For a moment, distracted by the beauty before me, I was able to quit worrying and just enjoy the snow. You could see every snowflake as it brushed the glass like angel wings. With my nose close to the glass like a 4-year-old, I focused on one snowflake after another, following its slow journey to the ground.

Then, just as suddenly as it had come, the snow suddenly stopped. It was warm enough that it melted quickly, and Justin was safely on his way to the game. From that moment on, whenever I start to get intimidated by the blizzard of illness circling around us on Cooper's long road to health, I would remind myself, "Just enjoy the snow."

With childlike abandon, I would try not to worry about what will happen in the future, but focus instead on the immense beauty in the moments at hand.

Sometimes that was harder than others, but I started to understand that if I could master the skill of "enjoying the snow," life would be filled with more joy and less worry. There is a Bible verse that says it perfectly: "This is the day that the Lord has made, let us rejoice and be glad in it." (Psalm 118:24)

Chapter Nineteen

Getting the Heck Out of Dodge

Cooper continued to improve, and they were able to take him off of one medication after another. Finally we started feeling that we were making progress. However, Cooper still needed several blood and platelet transfusions each week to maintain proper levels in his blood, so we remained in our "6th-floor penthouse," as we had come to call our hospital room. We joked that in New York this would be considered prime real estate.

Then one day our nurse with the spiked

hair walked into our room and announced, "Would you like to be unhooked from your tubies, Cooper?"

Justin and I looked at her in awe. Cooper had been hooked up to that IV pole for so long that we barely remembered what life was like without it. Now the doctor had given the orders to unhook Cooper, just like that. We couldn't believe it!

Cooper sat on the brown vinyl couch watching Tom and Jerry, ignoring the nurse while she worked. Nikki held on to the blue cap at the end of the tubes and twisted it, freeing our baby from his shackles. She flushed the line with heparin and said, "There you go!"

Surprised, Cooper looked at her and then down at his arm. He lifted his arm and then set it down again. For the first time in what seemed like forever, he could move without tubes flopping around and getting twisted up. He looked a little confused. Apparently even *he* had forgotten what it was like to be free of an IV pole, but He quickly adapted to the change.

A few days later, I ran to Target to get some things we needed. With Cooper unhooked and feeling better, I didn't feel so bad about leaving. Plus I knew Justin and he enjoyed their time together without me hovering. They usually snuck out for a walk in the halls, something I was glad to miss.

Cooper needed to get out of his room, but it stressed me out to let him walk just feet away from kids who had contagious illnesses that could kill him with his weakened immune system. Still, the doctors had said it was OK. They gave us permission to take Cooper walking around the halls and even outside on the patio, as long as he wore a mask. So I would leave, and Justin would put a mask on Cooper, and they would walk.

That day, while I was gone, the doctor and nurse practitioner took advantage of my absence to talk to Justin. They explained that even though Cooper's counts weren't recovering yet, he seemed to be stable, and they were considering discharging him to the Rainbow House, a Ronald McDonald-type house, a few blocks away. They felt Cooper might be exposed to fewer sick people and germs there rather than at the hospital while we waited for his body to recover.

They explained that we would need to come back to the hospital immediately if Cooper spiked a fever, but they felt we were very attentive parents, and they could trust us to do

that. As they talked to Justin, they admitted they were worried that I would be nervous to leave the hospital for fear that something bad would happen. So when I got back from shopping, Justin talked to me about it.

I looked at him incredulously at the notion that I would ever want to stay a moment longer at the hospital than necessary. He agreed, and we were both ecstatic at the prospect of escaping our medical prison.

While the doctors began the discharge process, I headed to the Rainbow House to get things ready. As I drove, I left the windows down in our blue minivan. The sun was out and the sky was blue – a picture-perfect day.

Cooper was admitted to the hospital on a cold February day, but now the seasons were changing. It was spring, and the air was starting to have some warmth to it. Birds were singing, flowers were blooming, and hope was in the air!

On my way, I swung by Target to get cleaning supplies and then followed Justin's directions to the Rainbow House. It was nicer than I imagined it might be. Justin had stayed there several nights, but I refused to leave the hospital for even one full night. Nights were sometimes rough for Cooper, and I always wanted to be right at hand if he needed me.

To my delight, upon check-in at the Rainbow House, I learned that we had been given the nicest room in the place. We would have a bedroom, bathroom, and family room. Compared to our tiny hospital room, it was a mansion!

To the average person, the room looked and smelled clean, but I was paranoid. Cooper's counts were still critically low, and I didn't want to take any chances, so I got to work cleaning away our invisible enemies. A few hours later, I finally emerged from the haze of Lysol and headed back to the hospital.

That evening, Cooper was finally discharged from the hospital. As we carried him out of his room, it seemed like we should be running before the doctors changed their minds.

As Justin buckled Cooper into his car seat, I couldn't help but think of the last time our son had sat there, his little body riddled with leukemia.

At that point, he had looked so healthy to the naked eye. We never would have guessed that 85% of the cells in his blood were cancerous. Now, with his beautiful, bald head, he was on the road to healing.

Chapter Twenty

The Rainbow House

As we pulled up in front of the Rainbow House, I dug around in my purse until I came up with one of the small masks they had sent along for Cooper to wear. The doctors told us it was a necessary precaution as long as Cooper's counts were low, as it would help protect him from anyone we may encounter that was sick.

As we walked into the Rainbow House, Justin and I started to feel the full weight of this huge responsibility settling down on our shoulders. It was getting late, so as soon as we arrived at our room, we gave the kids their baths. Cooper still had his PICC line (peripherally inserted central catheter) in place, so I gave him a sponge bath while Justin gave Tony a "real" bath.

At the hospital, I had become a sponge-bath expert. Our routine was a well-oiled machine. Here everything was different. Instead of an unlimited supply of towels, we were limited to one per person...for the week. There were no tubs to put the water in or soap easily at hand. Still, we got it figured out and finally passed the monumental milestone that was bath time at the Rainbow House.

Baths over, it occurred to us that we needed to go to the pharmacy for the medicine Cooper had to take that night. So Justin headed out.

By that point, it was 10 p.m., and we were all exhausted. I let the boys relax on our bed and watch a show while we waited for Justin to come back.

I turned and looked at the La-Z-Boy recliner in the room. At that moment, I realized that it had been 30 days since I last sat or laid on anything but stiff vinyl furniture. As I sank down into the softness of that old recliner, I felt like I had just re-entered the civilized world.

While I rested, I texted my mom and dad to let them know Cooper had been discharged from the hospital. They were in Albion, our hometown, attending a big fundraiser friends were throwing for our family.

The fundraiser was called "Baskets of Hope for Cooper." For weeks we had been watching on Facebook as they posted pictures of hundreds of baskets that had been donated from all over the United States. We would read each description with awe and marvel at the generosity of people.

We had initially hoped to be home for the fundraiser so that we could thank everyone, but that proved to be impossible, since Cooper's hospitalization had dragged on and on. My

parents were representing us that night.

When Mom received my text that we had moved into the Rainbow House, she went up on stage where the small band was playing and announced the good news. As if in a movie, the crowd erupted with cheers and applause.

Meanwhile, the scene in our little room that night was much more subdued, but just as filled with joy. When Justin got back, we carefully measured out the medicine. We had taken for granted how spoiled we were in the hospital when the nurses brought all Cooper's medications precisely on time and perfectly measured out for us in syringes.

We figured it out though, and then it was time for bed. Tony slept on the pullout sofa and Cooper was in his Pack-n-Play, reminding me of that last night at my parents' house before he was diagnosed. Both boys were quickly asleep, and I looked with overwhelming gratitude at their tiny little bodies as they lay breathing peacefully.

How many times had I taken this scene for granted? How much time had I wasted conjuring up things to worry about instead of being grateful for the miracles right before my eyes?

As I snuggled up to Justin in the bed that was actually big enough I could bend my knees, I thanked God for all the blessings I had previously taken for granted.

After a few days of living at the Rainbow House, Cooper's counts were finally high enough. The doctor said we could go home to Albion! It felt like that moment in the hospital, after your first child is born, when they walk you to your car. You wonder if they are sure they know what they are doing, allowing you to be in charge of such a fragile, precious little human. Still, you are profoundly grateful for the pure magic of the moment.

Chapter Twenty-One

Forty Days

As Justin drove us home, I turned and looked at Cooper in his car seat, his brother sitting next to him. Then, with awe, I looked at my husband and said, "Do you realize exactly 40 days ago we were on the other side of this highway with a very sick little boy?"

Forty days. For 40 days, the Israelites wandered in the desert, seeking the promise of God. For 40 days, Jesus was tempted and tested in the wilderness as the devil tried every last trick to bring Him down. For 40 days, we had fought our own demons and emerged on the other side, confident that God was with us through it all and would continue to stay by our side.

This journey was a long way from over for us. As Justin reminded me in the hospital, there will always be one more test. Still, we were grateful for all the miracles and support that were showered on us along the way. The next part of our lives was beginning, full of hope and love.

For further updates on our family's journey, visit www.genuflected.com/.

Our family: Justin, Tony, Cooper, and Jenni

Bald is beautiful.

Cuddling with BOTH my boys was such a treat!

Friends and family showered the boys with gifts.

We spent a lot of time snuggling.

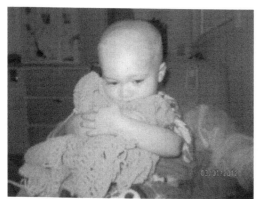

Sometimes a guy just needs his
favorite blanket, Greenie.

We were so happy when Cooper started to giggle
again.

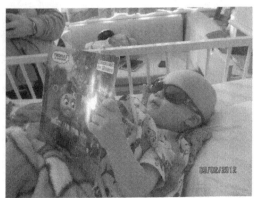
Cooper was keepin' it cool while
we waited to be discharged.

It's a good sign when they feel well enough to fight.

We rearranging the furniture
to fit our basketball needs.

Cooper quickly adjusted to life without an IV pole.

Cooper and Tony plotting their escape.

The first that day we arrived at Children's Hospital, Cooper and Tony were swinging from the bars under the crib. Our entire stay we said, "When Cooper feels well enough to swing from the crib again, we will know it's time to go home." That's exactly what happened!

Made in the USA
Charleston, SC
17 May 2016